BATHING
AND PLUNGE POOLS

Vivien Rolf

SHIRE PUBLICATIONS

Published in Great Britain in 2011 by Shire Publications Ltd, Midland House, West Way, Botley, Oxford OX2 0PH, United Kingdom.

44-02 23rd Street, Suite 219, Long Island City, NY 11101, USA.

E-mail: shire@shirebooks.co.uk   www.shirebooks.co.uk

A CIP catalogue record for this book is available from the British Library.

Shire Library no. 610.   ISBN-13: 978 0 74780 809 1

Vivien Rolf has asserted her right under the Copyright, Designs and Patents Act, 1988, to be identified as the author of this book.

Designed by Tony Truscott Designs, Sussex, UK and typeset in Perpetua and Gill Sans.

Printed in China through Worldprint Ltd.

11 12 13 14 15   10 9 8 7 6 5 4 3 2 1

COVER IMAGE
Detail from Rysbrack's painting of Lord Burlington's bagnio at Chiswick. The building provided a focal point in a theatrical setting and was influential in establishing a new garden fashion.

TITLE PAGE IMAGE
Dawlish Baths. (Westcountry Studies Library)

CONTENTS PAGE IMAGE
The 1760 bath house at Arnos Castle, Bristol. Threatened by a road-widening scheme, the façade was relocated to Portmeirion, Wales. The original elegant, plastered interior featuring waves, shells and dolphins did not survive.

ACKNOWLEDGEMENTS
My thanks go to family and friends who patiently joined me on many field trips to view bathing houses and plunge pools. Special thanks go to my technical support team for keeping me on track in times of stress. I am indebted to the Hon. Richard Curzon, the staff of Kedleston Hall, Derbyshire and Nikita Hooper of the National Trust Picture Library (NTPL) for their individual help in ensuring that Kedleston was included in this book. I also acknowledge my debt to the Building Recorders of the Devonshire Association and Wendy Osborne of the Friends of Anglesey Gardens whose enthusiasm for these buildings has retrieved them from obscurity.

Uncredited images are the author's own photographs.

Shire Publications is supporting the Woodland Trust, the UK's leading woodland conservation charity, by funding the dedication of trees.

CONTENTS

INTRODUCTION

THE VALUE of immersing the human body in water, whether for health, hygiene or pleasure, has been subject to sweeping cultural changes throughout British history. In the Ancient Roman Empire hot and cold public baths were enjoyed by both sexes, both separately and together. With the decline of the Empire, bathing, whether for health or hygiene, became the practice of the wealthy in privately owned baths. Medicinal baths, like those at Bath in Somerset, reflected changing fashions: from their heyday as a Roman centre for rest and relaxation, their subsequent decline and their renaissance from the twelfth century onwards to their huge success in Georgian England, their fluctuating popularity reflected changing ideas about the value of 'taking the waters'.

Crusaders returning to England brought back a fondness for the heated Turkish baths or *hamams* encountered abroad, and Londoners in the fourteenth century could take their pick from at least eighteen which existed there then. Although pilgrims had enjoyed cold or mineral waters at holy wells for their supposed healing properties, the Reformation drew a firm line under these relaxed attitudes to bathing, for whatever purpose. Frowning upon saintly miracles, nudity and overall contact between the human body and water (especially warm water), daily hygiene came generally to mean washing the hands and face only, and a regular change of linen in direct contact with the body to reduce offensive odours. These ideas were common to both rich and poor, although Queen Elizabeth I took a monthly bath at Windsor 'whether she needed it or no' (that is to say, whether she was in good health or bad, rather than dirty or clean).

If attitudes to cleanliness, even in high society, had not advanced significantly over the centuries, a new appreciation of the social possibilities of bathing began to emerge from the end of the seventeenth century. A group of Turkish merchants built an ambitious bath house in Newgate Street, London in 1679; it was octagonal in shape, with a central skylight, in the style of a *hamam*. The meteoric rise of Georgian Bath was mirrored by spa towns all over the country, wherever mineral springs could be harnessed for

Opposite:
The fishing pavilion at Kedleston, Derbyshire, giving a typically understated first impression, was dedicated to enjoyment and relaxation. (NTPL)

Lakeside view of the building on page 4, designed to impress and amaze. Robert Adam's creation at Kedleston epitomises the wealth and taste of Georgian aristocracy. Gaming, fishing and boating took place, with a plunge bath at water level. (NTPL)

the new fashion of drinking or bathing in the waters. Health theories centred on cold water baths became surprisingly popular in the eighteenth century with Dr Floyer and Dr Oliver both publishing treatises around 1700, aimed at an educated audience, and John Wesley's *Primitive Physick*, catering for a less educated readership and running to twenty-one editions. Swimming, as opposed to bathing, usually took place in lakes, ponds and rivers, as an alfresco summer activity. This was not without its hazards: the Bill of Mortality in a single year recorded 104 'melancholy accidents.' In 1742 and 1743, this informal style of swimming was superseded by two purpose-built pools in London, the *Bagnio* in Lemon Street and the Peerless Pool in Finsbury. The latter example was developed from a natural pond, recorded in 1603 as a favourite, though dangerous, place for bathing. The Pool evolved as a complex, offering both hot and cold baths, swimming lessons, model boating, fishing and winter ice skating, in addition to a bowling green and reading room, and was typical of the multiple uses to which both public and private baths were put. Although sea bathing took place in natural pools and bathing 'holes' around the coast, salt water bathing did not become generally popular until the 1750s. Into this patchwork of fluctuating attitudes to 'taking the waters' emerged an eighteenth-century fashion which took the aristocracy by storm, and altered the face of the great landscape gardens of the century – the fashion for the bathing house and the plunge pool.

The settled social order of the eighteenth century, combined with a booming economy, encouraged a great deal of investment in the large, country estates of the landed gentry, where estate 'improvements' became the order of the day. Wealthy landowners used these 'improvements' as indicators of wealth and taste, and nowhere was this more evident than in the landscapes which surrounded the newly fashionable Palladian mansions of the rich.

St Winifred's Well, Shropshire: visited by medieval pilgrims, it was later converted to a private plunge bath, and finally a public bath, which closed in 1755 because of 'riotous conduct' there. (Landmark Trust)

Plaster shellwork and a series of fish paintings point to the pavilion's dedication to watery pleasures. (Joanna Lowis/ National Trust)

The sculpture of Venus (right) and the relief of Venus reclining on a hippocamp (below) hint at the the pavilion's use for amorous pleasures. (Joanna Lowis/ National Trust)

By contrast, at lake level is the spartan, spring-fed plung pool. (Joanna Lowis/ National Trust)

Away from the mansion, small buildings began to appear, some purely decorative, some functional and some combining both aspects. Sham ruins, eye-catching follies and Greek temples were set in the landscape to enhance a view and demonstrate the owner's familiarity with the latest architectural fashions. Functional buildings such as ice houses and game larders served a practical purpose, but were often of a decorative nature. Bathing houses and plunge pools seem to fall midway between the two categories, since they served a practical purpose in providing somewhere for the landowner to indulge in the latest method of 'taking the waters', as well as providing what was often a secluded venue for outings and small-scale social gatherings.

At its simplest, a plunge pool might be no more than a small, shallow, open-air pool utilising a nearby spring for the water supply. Sometimes a nearby grotto or a small, rustic building served as a changing room before the owner bathed naked, as was the fashion, to improve his health. These simple open-air provisions were usually private, although public bathing took place on Hampstead Heath in London in ponds dug as reservoirs in the seventeenth century. More ambitious plunge pools might be contained within a bath house, often built to demonstrate the latest architectural fashion such as Gothick or picturesque, and hot and cold baths were often provided, together with a steam room. Occasionally a bath house building might also house a model dairy to provide an occupation for the ladies (after the style of Marie Antionette) while the gentlemen recreated the bath house pleasures of Ancient Rome.

Kedleston Hall in Derbyshire shows the evolving fashions, with sulphur baths being opened to the public in the grounds around 1759 as a business venture, and achieving success as a miniature spa. A private fishing pavilion was later designed for the estate by Robert Adam in 1770. Dedicated to Venus, the pavilion contained a fishing and gaming room, with twin boathouses and a freshwater plunge pool below.

The sulphur baths at Kedleston, constructed in 1759. (Author photograph/ National Trust)

FORERUNNERS OF FASHION

ALTHOUGH increasingly relaxed religious ideas, together with new medical theories, brought about a fashion for bathing houses and plunge pools during the eighteenth century, they were not an entirely new idea in Britain, and two Scottish bathing houses survive from the late sixteenth and early seventeenth centuries. Opinion varies about the exact use of the building known as Queen Mary's Bath House at Holyrood Palace in Edinburgh. Variously described as a garden pavilion, summer house or a dovecot, legend has it that Mary bathed there in sweet white wine. Under house arrest in later life at New Hall in Buxton, she enjoyed regular warm mineral baths there. A member of the Scottish Privy Council of Queen Mary's son James VI, Sir David Lindsay may have had Queen Mary's Bath House in mind when he began to create a unique garden at Edzell Castle in Scotland in 1604. The bath house there was destroyed during the 1745 Jacobite rising, leaving only the footings, but its twin, the summer house, remains to demonstrate Sir David's grasp of Italian Renaissance ideas in providing such impressive places of retreat for family and guests.

Edzell's achievement is all the more remarkable because it predates Sir Francis Bacon's influential essay *Of Gardens* by twenty years. A high achiever, Bacon was Queen Elizabeth I's Lord Chancellor before falling from grace. Philosopher, scientist, statesman and essayist, he had firm views on what a garden should contain. A lover of fountains, he disliked still pools of water, which made 'the garden unwholesome, full of flies and frogs.' The cold bath, however, was an essential accessory, on condition that it contained 'no rust, mossiness, putrefaction, fish, slime or mud.' Some 30 to 40 feet square, it needed to be cleaned by hand each day, have steps up to the pool and fine pavements surrounding it, with the sides and bottom of the pool also finely paved. Most importantly the water that fed it should be in perpetual motion.

While Edzell Castle reflected the fashions of Renaissance Italy, Albury Park in Surrey was influenced by a much earlier period of Italian history. Thomas Howard, Earl of Arundel, retreated to Italy in self-imposed exile during the English Civil War, to be joined there by his friend, the diarist

Opposite:
The ornately carved and decorated walls at Edzell displaying their owner's taste and education. At the furthest point from the castle, at either end of the boundary wall, were the summer and bath houses. (Crown copyright. Courtesy of Historic Scotland, www.historicscotlandimages.gov.uk)

A series of narrow grass terraces descend from Albury House to the River Tillingbourne before the steeply rising land leads the eye up to the yew walk, the terraces above and woodland at the hill's summit. (Courtesy of the Albury Estate)

John Evelyn, and his grandson Henry, later 6th Duke of Norfolk. Recreating their impressions from this prototype Grand Tour, Albury Park references the presumed site of Virgil's tomb at Posilippo near Naples. In the Surrey downland Henry and Evelyn created a 'memory theatre' of their exile.

Steps in the lower terrace descended into the plunge pool, roughly 5 metres square and 1 metre deep when full of water, under a curved brick roof, with eleven statue niches set into the surrounding walls. Immediately above was the large pool backed by the *exedra*, with a tunnel about 50 metres long running off at right angles through the hillside to give a view across the scenery below on the other side of the hill, in imitation of the *crypta* at Posilippo. Albury recreated the Arcadian scenes which the exiles would have seen around Naples, reflecting the lost golden age of classical Italian

civilisation. The garden was a favourite metaphor of seventeenth-century English poets and writers for the sense of lost innocence resulting from the turmoil of the English Civil War. Lord Arundel rated Albury Park above all his other possessions, with the exception of Arundel itself. John Evelyn's

Set as a central 'eye-catcher' in the lower terrace is the entrance to a subterranean Roman style brick-built bath house – Lord Arundel's *thermae*. (Courtesy of the Albury Estate)

Set in the terrace above the bath house, a semi-circular pool and fountain fed from the nearby Silent Pool in Albury village, with water running from the upper pool though a conduit into the bath below. (Courtesy of the Albury Estate)

view that 'caves, grotts, mounts, and irregular ornaments of gardens do contribute to contemplative and philosophical enthusiasme' shows that in previous ages garden buildings were expected to have aesthetic as well as practical uses.

An exact contemporary of Albury, but in a completely different vein is Packwood House and gardens in Warwickshire. The acquisition of Packwood marked the transition from yeomen to gentlemen for the Fetherstons. Inheriting the estate in 1670, Thomas Fetherston built the plunge bath in Fountain Court in 1680, alongside the main entrance to the house. The plunge pool is completely open to the elements and lacks any convenient changing room close by. Since the habit of the period was to bathe naked, the pool is surprisingly open to the casual gaze of any passer-by; the surrounding hedge provides only a modest amount of cover. A sluice gate on the lake

William Cobbett in 1822 described a row of small yew trees, and the terraces, a quarter of a mile long, 30 or 40 feet wide, and 10 feet high. (Courtesy of the Albury Estate)

controls the water supply to the plunge pool, where it feeds through an ornamental water faucet bearing the arms of the family. Steep steps lead down into the pool and the water drains away when a paddle beside the water faucet is lifted. Thomas's father was a martyr to gout, referring to 'the payne and greif' of his illness; maybe Thomas installed the plunge pool in the hope of averting the ailment.

Edzell, Albury and Packwood are three different types of plunge pools, created for very different reasons, but they all advertised the status of their owners: Edzell built to impress visitors with Sir David Lindsay's erudition and style; Albury Park built as a memento of a period in Italy immersed in an ancient civilisation before the Grand Tour became *de rigeur*; and Packwood as a sign that its owner had reached the status of a gentleman who aspired to set a fashion for the coming age.

Packwood plunge. The original carriage drive to the house lay along the causeway of an ornamental lake feeding the plunge pool. Thomas Fetherston was proud enough of the plunge pool to site it prominently in view of every visitor to the house. (Author photograph/ National Trust)

ARCHITECTS OF THE NEW ORDER

S EVENTEENTH-CENTURY uncertainties, including civil war and regicide, were replaced by the Hanoverian monarchy, thirty years of parliamentary Whig domination and a booming economy. A settled order and a surplus of money encouraged the aristocracy once more to invest in estate 'improvement'. Similarly, a growing middle class expressed their new-found wealth and taste in the acquisition of property and land. 'Taste' and 'sensibility', two key words of the eighteenth century, were revealed by a man's knowledge of the classical world, and a classical education marked a gentleman out from the lesser orders. A wave of neo-classical mansions replaced the baroque architectural fashions of a previous age; these mansions, and the temples and grottoes in the landscape gardens surrounding them, displayed their owners' familiarity with the classical world. Vast quantities of statuary, paintings and *objets d'art* were shipped back to England to enrich the new-style mansions and their surrounding gardens.

First amongst these new improvers was the wealthy young Richard Boyle, 3rd Lord Burlington, who made several long visits to Italy between 1714 and 1720. In the Palladian-style buildings he saw there, he recognised a suitable signature style for the new Augustan age of civilisation in which the English aristocracy thought they were living. Together with William Kent, whom he met in Italy, Burlington proved a huge influence on garden design. Kent was the polar opposite of the wealthy and aristocratic Burlington, but despite his humble origins he grasped the opportunities which Burlington's wealth and patronage afforded him, and as a member of Burlington's household, moved freely amongst royalty and nobility, introducing to their estates ideas of a more natural, less regimented style.

Arriving back in England with 878 trunks of art purchases after his 1714 tour, Burlington began to reshape the gardens of his Chiswick estate with ideas gleaned from abroad. The *Bagnio* served as an 'eye-catcher' at the end of a gravel pathway between high, clipped yew hedges, and was part of the *patte d'oie* or 'goose foot' formed of three such radiating paths, each terminating at a different garden building. It was a substantial building, with

Opposite: Kent's sketch for an unrealised classical plunge pool at Chatsworth. (Devonshire Collection, Chatsworth by permission of Chatsworth Settlement Trustees)

a frontage measuring approximately 10 metres. Four rooms occupied the ground floor, with a spacious saloon above, and the cold bath, fed with water from the Bollo Brook, was probably housed in the basement. Drawings suggest that one room was fitted out as a bedroom, and the building also contained a library and drawing office where Burlington could work at his new enthusiasm for architecture. The age of the aristocratic bath house had now arrived.

Two commissions by William Kent established him as a garden designer: his input with other gardeners at Stowe, and also at Carlton House. Bath houses existed on both sites, but neither remains today. Kent's work on both of these projects was highly praised and reported,

Above: Grotto Grande, Pitti Palace, Florence. A rite of passage for young aristocrats, the Grand Tour inspired the buildings they created on their return home.

Right: Lord Burlington, painted c. 1717 in front of the *bagnio* ('bath') or *casina* ('little house') in the gardens of Chiswick House, designed in collaboration with Colen Campbell. (National Portrait Gallery, London)

but Carlton House proved more influential. Abundant and luxurious plantings of trees and flowers there concealed any sense of being in a relatively small town garden. Kent's *bagnio*, designed in 1734 for Frederick, Prince of Wales, was set across lawns from Carlton House, and was an exuberant octagonal building with the bath behind an arched ground-floor opening, and stairways sweeping up to give access to the domed saloon above.

Kent's work for General Dormer on the house and gardens at Rousham in Oxfordshire survives virtually unaltered today. Kent built on the previous layout there by Charles Bridgeman, composing a series of arranged surprises focusing attention on natural views, statuary and purpose-built garden structures. The garden visitor was intended to wander from one viewpoint to the next, pausing to sit and ponder on the view that Kent presented. In Horace Walpole's view it was at Rousham that Kent 'leapt the fence and saw that all nature was a garden', working to encompass the surrounding countryside as the background to a series of picturesque scenes. While Rousham understandably commands a great deal of respect in gardening history, Kent may also have brought his irreverent sense of humour into play there. Not much given to committing himself in writing, Kent left a body of drawings and designs behind which provide some clue to his character. A strong element of the fantastic is mixed in some sketches with the decidedly earthy, where dogs and men relieve themselves with apparent unconcern amid classical temples and obelisks.

One of several Rysbrack paintings showing the *bagnio* complex, which Burlington often used as an alternative dining venue to Chiswick House. The bathing house in this view can be seen in more detail on the cover. (English Heritage Photographic Library)

Statues of Venus, Bacchus and Pan suggest a pagan engagement with the delights of life. (By permission of C. Cottrell Dormer)

Today, the stonework of the statuary at Rousham has weathered, as would be expected over centuries, but originally many of the statues were painted in realistic flesh tones. It must have been a disconcerting experience to turn a bend in a woodland path and come upon a naked and shapely representation of the human body. The open-air octagonal plunge pool at Rousham lies in just such a wooded glade, the pool constantly fed through a stone rill with water from the River Cherwell, which ensured that bathing there must always have been a Spartan experience. A minute Gothic stonework grotto serves as a changing room to one side of the path, but there is no fireplace there to warm the bather after his plunge.

The plunge pool at Rousham. Coming unexpectedly across someone emerging from the plunge pool, it could have seemed that one of General Dormer's painted statues had come to life and felt the need to cool off. (By permission of C. Cottrell Dormer)

A similar engagement with pleasure seems to have been the inspiration for the building at Carshalton in Surrey which its owner, Sir John Fellowes, described modestly as 'the greenhouse and *bagnio* at the bottom of the

Chosen for its proximity to the City of London and the famed purity of its water supply, Carshalton House was in the Queen Anne style. (By permission of the Trustees and Friends of Carshalton Water Tower Trust)

The water tower complex had to be strong enough to accommodate the weight of the water tank and the giant wheel that pumped up the water. (Carshalton Water Tower Trust)

Interior
of the *bagnio*.
(Carshalton Water
Tower Trust)

garden'. Charles Bridgeman was the designer of the original garden layout there, having also undertaken commissions at Chiswick, Stowe and Rousham. Designed to showcase Sir John's new wealth from banking, the water tower complex, fed from the River Wandle, lay across lawns, a ha-ha and an ornamental canal, and must have been the envy of all visitors. An underground spring provided the water which was pumped up by a giant water wheel into the lead cistern on the top of the tower, supplying the *bagnio* below and Carshalton House itself. No doubt would-be investors invited to enjoy Sir John's hospitality would have been impressed by this display of solid wealth. Work probably began on the brick-built complex around 1718, with the building housing a saloon, pump chamber, orangery, *bagnio* and robing room. The west-facing saloon looks across the park to the mansion, and was probably used as a destination for gaming, conversation, wine drinking and small social gatherings, or as a resting place on walks along the perimeter of the estate between the Folly

A trio of niches
fills the east wall
of the *bagnio* with
a door to the
robing room
alongside,
complete with
fireplace.
(Carshalton Water
Tower Trust)

Bridge and the Hermitage. Measuring 3.26 metres by 2.6 metres and 1.37 metres deep, the north-facing *bagnio* is entered by a short flight of white Carrara marble steps. The larger-than-average proportions allowed room for luxurious immersion for one occupant, or, more possibly, the opportunity for several people to bathe together. Carrara marble, together with black slate, was also used to form the square-patterned floor of the bath and surround. Cold water was used, and, possibly, sometimes warm or scented water.

Lancelot (Capability) Brown came to Stowe gardens in 1740, inheriting the legacy of William Kent's influential designs there. Rising to become Head Gardener, he was given the opportunity to develop useful contacts with wealthy and influential potential clients. He developed a style of landscape

Delft-style tiles patterned in blue and magenta bear variations on the theme of a vase of flowers, with stylised carnation motifs in each corner.
(Carshalton Water Tower Trust)

Close by the lake lies one of several buildings Lancelot (Capability) Brown designed to improve the gardens of Burghley House – the bath house, known also as the banqueting house, complete with underfloor heating. (Burghley House Collection)

As a tribute
to Burghley's
sixteenth-century
architecture,
Brown drew on
the Jacobean style
of the banqueting
houses at Chipping
Campden with
their openwork
parapets and
'fantastick'
chimneys at each
corner, like giant
sticks of candy
surmounted by
openwork
pinnacles.
(Landmark Trust)

design which appeared entirely natural, but in reality often required vast amounts of structural work in terms of earth shifting, re-routing of roads, flooding of valleys and the occasional re-siting of a village. In 1756 Brown began a 25-year working relationship with the Earl of Exeter's Burghley estates in Lincolnshire, which only ended when Brown died. Brown converted the meandering streams at Burghley into a 32-acre lake, ornamented at one point by a bath house with under-floor heating. This building was used also as a banqueting house – a destination at this period for wine, desserts and sweetmeats after a heavy meal had been taken in the dining room of the main house, while the company relaxed and enjoyed the view.

Brown was also responsible for the Gothick bathing house and plunge pool at Corsham Court in Wiltshire, where he worked on alterations to the house and gardens from 1760. Reached through a doorway in a high wall, the bather travelled along a gloomy, serpentine corridor, emerging at the rear of the plunge pool to delight in the view across the pleasure grounds. Although these buildings were designed to facilitate a cold plunge, stylistically they are far removed from the craggy grottoes of Stourhead and Twickenham, and

Stamford Public
Bath House.
On the site of an
earlier bath house,
built by four local
surgeons in 1722,
the Marquis of
Exeter (owner of
Burghley House)
created this public
gothick bath house
in 1823.

the rigours of Rousham. Charming, fairytale, small-scale buildings set in manicured lawns, Corsham and Burghley seem dedicated to pleasure rather than pensive reflection and melancholy.

Ascribing estates as the work of Capability Brown can pose problems where documentation is scanty or absent, but Warnford Park in Hampshire has many of his signature trademarks, and the bathing house

In front of the bath house at Corsham Court there was originally a pear-shaped lake, created during Capability Brown's improvements. (By permission of J. Methuen Campbell)

Just as romantic as Burghley, the bathing house at Corsham Court, with steps down into a stone plunge pool, and a dressing room on the floor above. (By permission of J. Methuen Campbell)

bears a close resemblance to an unexecuted Brown design for a lakeside lodge at Rothley in Northumberland. A bathing house existed at Warnford in 1760, but may originally have been simply an octagonal gazebo above the plunge pool, possibly open-sided and of timber construction. John de Burgh, 11th Earl of Clanricarde, and his son Henry were responsible for transforming the estate and creating the current bathing house. Correspondence in 1773 resulted in a survey by Brown's son-in law, and the renaming of the estate as Belmont. The *Morning Post* of 29 September 1789 describes 'the ugly Gothic building with the bath under it of Lady Mary'. In the tradition of Corsham and Burghley, Warnford's bathing house looks like a fantasy dolls' house in a secluded position, overlooking the end of the parkland. Water meadows, long pre-dating Brown's work, drew on supplies from the River Meon, running through Warnford Park. The system was harnessed to supply the bathing house, with sluice gates controlling the flow of water into an octagonal collecting pool, and holding it until a sufficient body of water accumulated and was released through a second sluice gate, along a grassy canal into the subterranean bath, emptying out again into the ornamental lake just beyond the bathing house. In common with many buildings on country estates, the bathing house changed its purpose over time. When the fashion for cold baths faded, this building was enlarged and became the Dower House, firstly for Urania, Lady Clanricarde, until eventually being downgraded to the gardener's cottage.

Warnford's bathing house. Viewed from the front, the building appears to be of a single storey set on a grassy mound. (By permission of W. Thuillier)

Left: The plunge bath was entered through a grotto tunnel.
(By permission of W. Thuillier)

Below: Viewed from the side, it becomes clear that three storeys exist astride the canal, one partly submerged below ground in the canal.
(By permission of W. Thuillier)

Nymph of the grot these sacred springs I keep
And to the murmur of these waters sleep
Ah spare my slumbers gently tread the cave
And drink in silence or in silence lave

A P

POPE'S GROTTO AND STOURHEAD

ALEXANDER POPE, the poet, another of Burlington's protégés, acted as advisor on the new-style garden at Chiswick. Together Pope, Burlington and Kent visited, sketched, planned and 'improved' the estates of the influential, disseminating ideas about the latest fashions. By 1719, Pope had earned enough from his translation of the *Iliad* to leave Burlington's household and build his own villa on the Thames at Twickenham. Refining all the ideas he had practised on other estates, and utilising his own advice to 'Consult the Genius of the Place' in designs, Pope produced a unique garden. Bordered on one side by lawns to the Thames, Pope's house was built hard up against the London to Hampton Court road on the other side, allowing no area for private gardens. Pope overcame this with a tunnel under the house and the London Road, creating private gardens beyond. Dr Johnson commented sharply:

> [His] excavation was requisite as an entrance to his garden, and as some men try to be proud of their defects, he extracted an ornament from an inconvenience, and vanity produced a grotto where necessity enforced a passage.

Johnson was no fan of grottoes, whereas Pope was, describing his own elaborate example:

> A luminous room, a Camera obscura; on the walls of which the objects of the River, Hills, Woods, and Boats are forming a moving picture in their visible Radiations: And when you have a mind to light it up, it affords you a very different Scene; it is finished with Shells interspersed with Pieces of Looking-glass in angular forms…and when a lamp…is hung in the Middle, a thousand pointed Rays glitter and are reflected over the Place.

In Homeric tradition, the Muses lived in caves where springs rose, hence Pope's depiction of his grotto as a '*Musaeum*' where inspiration came for his literary work.

Opposite:
The sleeping Ariadne guards the source of the Stour above Pope's words: 'Nymph of the grot these sacred springs I keep, And to the murmur of these waters sleep, Ah! Spare my slumbers, gently tread the cave, And drink in silence, or in silence lave.'
(NTPL)

During the excavations for the tunnel, a spring was discovered 'which falls in a perpetual rill that echoes thro' the Cavern day and night', and a *bagnio* was added to the attractions of Pope's 'pensive grot'. Suffering from a spinal deformity caused by tuberculosis, Pope may have subscribed to beliefs in the health-giving properties of a cold plunge bath. Pope's garden was a much-visited legend in his own lifetime and beyond, and provided inspiration for William Kent, whose sketches of the garden survive today. Pope's house was demolished in 1807 by the owner, Baroness Sophia Charlotte Howe, 'Queen of the Goths', who was reportedly exasperated by the constant stream of visitors to the site.

Stourhead, too, was the inspired work of the amateur – Henry Hoare II, who set out from 1743 to create a continuous scenic commentary in the landscape, with the lake as the central focus. The second generation of a banking family, Hoare's gardens at Stourhead established his credentials as a man of taste. A major tourist attraction from its inception, it became one of the most visited landscapes in England. The gardens could be enjoyed at many levels by visitors, but for Hoare's peers in terms of wealth and land-holding, the references and symbolism of the garden buildings were meant to display the owner's intimate knowledge of Virgil's *Aeneid*. The iconography at Stourhead is at its most complex in the grotto with its cold plunge bath, embracing classical, pagan and Christian, with the view artfully contrived to resemble a landscape painting by Gaspard Dughet.

This is a description by Henry Hoare's grandson:

[We] are conducted by a well-planned approach, to the Grotto…in the construction of which nature seems to have been consulted in preference to art; here we see no finery, no shells, no crystals, no variety of fossils collected together, but the native stone, forming natural stalactites, and the *aquae dulces vivoque sedilia saxo* (sweet waters and seats of living rocks) compose the interior of the cavern; the sombre appearance of which is relieved by two figures very appropriately placed....

Stourhead is an experience very different from the comforts of Carshalton and more akin to the bath chamber being built at the same period at Walton, but with a complex additional iconography missing from many bath houses. An inscription set in the edge of the cold bath is a translation by Pope of a pseudo-classical poem, intended for his grotto at Twickenham, on which Stourhead is believed to have been modelled.

The Christian iconography of the medieval Bristol High Cross and Stourton Church was only properly visible from the plunge pool or one of the low rockwork niches either side. (NTPL)

MRS DELANEY AND THE WALTON BATH HOUSE

W ALTON combines all the elements so dear to the heart of the cultured, landed gentry of that period, allowing the landowner to demonstrate his familiarity with fashionable ideas in architecture and health, and also with the burgeoning interest in the natural world and the landscape. Sir Charles Mordaunt's plans for a grand bath house in the woodland above the approach drive to Walton Hall must have provided plenty of enjoyable planning and discussion with like-minded landed gentry, all busy improving their estates in the booming economy of the period. In an area boasting impressive achievements such as Compton Verney, Farnborough and Hagley Hall, Sir Charles left his mark on the landscape at a relatively small expense, whilst demonstrating his familiarity with the fashionable concerns of the *dilettanti*. He was probably aided in this scheme by his friendship with the gentleman architect Sanderson Miller, who was an amateur designer of Gothic follies and 'ruins' for his friends at this time. Although the entire project was not finished until 1755, Miller's accounts for 1749 suggest that the fabric of the building was nearing completion then by one of his own servants, William Hitchcox, who combined the role of valet to Miller with that of stonemason on some of his building projects.

Set amongst trees just below the Roman Fosse Way, on a steep slope where springs rise from the ground, the ground floor, housing the plunge bath, is composed of large, rough-hewn stones, suggesting a cave in a hillside, with the plunge bath situated behind a curved entrance, open to the elements. Rough stone pillars support a curved rockwork canopy above the bath, with a set of small steps leading into a plunge pool approximately 3.5 metres square. Bats roost within the bath vault, and birds, deer and rabbits come to feed in the glade below the building. This landscape combined all the elements for a society newly enthused by natural history and the environment. A flight of uneven steps set into the rock cliff face behind the plunge pool give access to the drawing room above. Creating a visual surprise beloved of the period, the watery nature of the plunge bath below the drawing room is echoed in the room above by plasterwork

Opposite:
Walton bath house, Warwickshire. One of the finest and best documented bathing houses still remaining from the eighteenth century, where the contrast between the craggy, rough-hewn rock setting of the pool is in deliberate contrast to the ordered, Palladian style above.
(Landmark Trust)

Above: Non-committal and unrevealing, the main door to the sitting room opens immediately onto a second door to prolong the suspense before the romantic interior is revealed.

Above right and right: With its architectural references in the housing of the cold plunge bath to the grottoes of ancient civilisation and Renaissance Italy, and the elegant Palladian style of the upper drawing room, the building encompasses some of the major trends to be found on the estates of those who would have called themselves 'polite society' or 'men of sensibility'. (Landmark Trust)

decorations 'to represent a wall worn by water-drops, with icicles sticking to it', and with decorative festoons of exotic sea shells enlivening the walls, as though 'some invisible sea nymph or triton placed them there for their private amusement.'

Georgian symmetry defines the upper building, with two minute lobbies either side of the main entrance door. One of the lobbies leads down stone steps, through a rustic wooden door into the plunge bath below. The bath house would not have been visible from Walton Hall, being approached through

What marks Walton out from many other bathing houses is the unexpected beauty of the drawing room's decoration.

woodland, so that the visitor would come upon the back, upstairs entrance suddenly, without warning, to a building offering no hint of its purpose. This mysterious introduction to the bath house, which offers no clue to the splendours within or watery delights below, was common to many bathing houses and similar surprises can be found at Kedleston, Greenway and Antony.

Natural springs feed the plunge pool and the bather's view looks onto an Arcadian landscape untroubled by civilisation.

The first mention of the interior decoration of the drawing room occurs in 1754, when Mrs Mary Delaney writes from Ireland to her sister, Mrs Anne Dewes at Wellesbourne, a neighbouring estate to Walton. Descendants of the previously rich and influential Granville family, Mary and Anne could still boast impeccable antecedents, even if the emergence of the Hanoverian monarchy had weakened the family's favoured position in court circles. Born in 1700 and living until 1788, Mary Delaney chronicled much of her age in extensive correspondence; friendships with Jonathan Swift, Handel, John Wesley and David Garrick reflected her lively interest in literature, music, religion and the theatre. Her second marriage to Dean Patrick Delaney enabled her to move amongst society around Dublin, mixing with the great aristocratic families, where her opinion on the decorative arts was eagerly sought. Her letters reflect the constant requests to advise landowners on their estate and garden improvements, and to provide schemes for enhancing both stately homes and the follies and grottoes that were then the height of fashion within the landscape.

Doubtless the Delaneys' own *ferme ornée* at Delville proved an inspiration to many of their society friends who visited them there and admired the grotto, the temple, the beggar's hut, the menagerie and the cold bath house.

Mrs Delaney made long visits from Dublin to her sister at Wellesbourne, meeting with the architect Sanderson Miller in 1753. This may have laid the seeds for a request that she decorate the Walton bath

Right and opposite top: The overall effect in the drawing room of being within an enchanted, aqueous cavern is heightened by the gentle, persistent sound of water merging from the rock face into the plunge bath below. (Landmark Trust)

Opposite bottom: Diana Reynell and her assistant working on the restoration of the bath house for the Landmark Trust, showing the variety and complexity of the shell swags. (Landmark Trust)

house, for by July 1754 her letters comment that the shell festoons to decorate the walls there could not be made by her in Ireland and shipped to England but must be made *in situ* at Walton. Shells gathered both in Ireland and brought for the purpose from the West Indies, Naples and the Channel Islands were packed into barrels and transported by sea, eventually arriving in Warwickshire, where they were made up into swag-shaped festoons mounted on wooden boards and then set into the plaster walls of the upper room at the bath house. The shell swags seem to have been a group effort by Mrs Delaney and her sister, together with Sir Charles's two daughters. Mrs Delaney was at pains to gather large and impressive shells such as conches and giant clams to 'make considerable figure enough' so

that their effect would not be lost when mounted 3 metres up on the walls. Further concerns were expressed when Sanderson Miller's plasterer, Robert Moore, started work on the plaster icicles which adorn the

ceiling, and anxious correspondence took place over how the eventual plan of thousands of icicles cascading down the domed octagonal ceiling would look in relation to the shell swags below.

Thanks to the painstaking restoration by the Landmark Trust after years of vandalism, it is possible once again to enjoy the magical and romantic experience that visiting the bath house must have been: the quiet path through the bluebell woods where only birdsong broke the silence, and then the arrival at the enigmatic and mysterious entrance with no hint at the fantasy created within. Sir Charles Mordaunt left no record of his use of the cold bath house, but his nephew wrote from Naples, entering into the element of fantasy that permeates the bath house by imagining that he might rub a magic ring and be transported to Walton to be an invisible guest at the tea parties that took place in the drawing room.

CHANGING
FASHIONS

IN 1750 Doctor Richard Russell gave new impetus to the health fashion for a cold plunge with his theory on the benefits of salt water bathing. Russell's *Dissertation on the Use of Sea-Water in Diseases of the Glands, particularly, the Scurvy, Jaundice, King's Evil, Leprosy and the Glandular Consumption* was greeted enthusiastically, turning Brighton from a rustic fishing village into a smart seaside resort enjoying royal patronage. The new fashion also encouraged a new generation of bathing houses and plunge pools on coasts and salt water estuaries. The fashion for taking a cold plunge bath was about to be re-invented.

In 1720 the 2nd Duke of Montagu planned a new commercial venture on the Beaulieu River in Hampshire, to be known as Montagu Town. A free port for the import and export of sugar, this was an adventurous project, including all the usual buildings to be found within a busy quay, but, unusually, also including provision for two sea baths. Reaching no further than the drawing board, the area developed instead as the shipyard known today as Buckler's

Beaulieu bath house: in a coppice of oaks, this fairy-tale cottage may once have housed an indoor warm plunge pool. Today, an open-air salt water pool still exists in the garden, overlooking the river. (By permission of the Beaulieu Estate)

Hard. The Duke, renowned as a very early Gothic revivalist, died in 1749, but a small part of his plans was realised by the next generation when a salt water plunge pool and bathing house was built close by for George, Duke of Montagu in 1760.

Filling at high water through a culvert under the river bank, a heavy tidal flap prevents the water running back out into the river as the twice-daily tide drops. Although an inconvenient 2 miles distant from Beaulieu Abbey itself, the Duke's Bath House is sited to take advantage of the salinity of the water at this point. The choice of location may also have exhibited the new enthusiasm for Romanticism in the landscape.

Contemporary with Dr Russell's theory were new ideas about the appreciation of beauty to be found within nature. An enthusiasm for alpine crags and rocky ravines, brooding lakes and mysterious forests all flourished as a reaction to the rationality of the Age of Enlightenment. Edmund Burke's *A Philosophical Enquiry into the Origin of Our Ideas of the Sublime and Beautiful* explored the differing emotional responses evoked by landscapes. Smooth lawns, gentle slopes and graceful groups of trees were classified as beautiful; totally in keeping with the ordered symmetry of the neo-classical architecture that dominated taste in the early eighteenth century. By contrast, the fashion for the sublime style, more in keeping with the Romanticism of the late eighteenth century, admired vistas that evoked emotions such as awe, wonder and dread. Burke's ideas were translated into the landscape gardens of the rich and influential, where rocky glens, foaming cascades and ruined stone 'eye catchers' began to appear. Landowners with river or sea frontages to their estates were able to take advantage of both Russell's and Burke's

Lord Churston's bathing house at Elbury Cove, Brixham. The walls of the building, now ruined, reveal fireplace recesses and a flue system, possibly to provide sauna facilities in addition to the warm sea water baths taken here as late as 1936. (B. Rolf)

39

A 1950s postcard shows the beach no longer privately owned, and the bathing house, damaged by vandalism, with the roof being dismantled. (B. Rolf)

theories when building themselves a new bathing house to adorn their estate. Beaulieu may be an early example of this fashion, where anyone bathing in the open air plunge pool would have felt himself part of an untamed landscape composed of a sweeping river, bordered only by reed beds and mature trees.

Nowhere is the diversity of style and usage of these second-generation bathing houses more apparent than in four Devon bathing houses, which reveal the tastes and aspirations of their owners, linked to the fashions of the day. Lord Churston's bathing house at Elbury Cove, Brixham, enjoyed a long life, first appearing on a map in 1835 and remaining in use for a century more when the dowager Lady Churston took warm seawater baths there to ease her rheumatoid arthritis. Probably built around 1803 when Sir Francis Yarde-Buller was improving his estate at Churston Ferrers, the bathing house was a three-storey stone construction perched on rocks rising out of the sea. With a thatched roof, whitewashed stucco walls and a large, picture window looking across Torbay, the building offers few clues as to its purpose. Inside the bath house at sea level, steps led down into a small, brick-lined circular plunge bath, fed directly at high tide with seawater through a wall grating. The experience of using the plunge pool must have been similar to that of descending into a shallow well. Above an intervening floor (possibly a changing room) lies the room with the view, used for lunches and picnics until the mid-twentieth century. At some later stage an extension was made to the rear of the building to house a large boiler, water tank and fuel store. Sea bathing and sailing were also enjoyed here by family and visitors at Churston Ferrers. Visitors would have experienced that element of mystery common to many bathing houses, with the building being approached along a narrow footpath through shady woodland which emerged suddenly onto a secluded beach with the bath house looking across the whole of Torbay.

Close by, as the crow flies, is the Greenway estate on the River Dart, with a building known misleadingly as Sir Walter Raleigh's boathouse. Agatha Christie, who bought the estate in 1938 wrote:

> We went over to Greenway, and very beautiful the house and grounds were. A white Georgian house of 1780 or 1790, with woods sweeping down to the Dart below, and lots of fine trees and shrubs – the ideal house, a dream house…

Built around 1791, the two-storey bathing house contained a rectangular plunge pool on the ground floor, with a drawing room upstairs. The single-storey boathouse alongside is a later addition to what was, originally, a thatched building. The plunge pool within filled at high water directly from the river through three arched apertures in the stone jetty. The balcony and wood cladding may have been Victorian additions, contemporary with the removal of the thatched roof, since, stripped of these and the boathouse, the building is much more in line with the architectural tastes of the 1790s, and its rustic symmetry would have been worthy of a Palladian design for a Tuscan farm building. Bathing in the plunge pool must have been a rather gloomy experience, since the lunette windows allow little light to enter, and no attempt was made to engage with the beautiful views outside. At some point metal shutters were fitted over the water inlets to the pool so that bathing would have been possible at all states of the tide.

Greenway. Attempts to restore the pool for use by Agatha Christie's family proved unrewarding, since the water showed a disappointing tendency to drain away of its own accord. The author used the bath house as the scene of a murder in a thriller, *Dead Man's Folly*. (National Trust/ Jo Unwin)

Undoubtedly the grandest of the Dart bathing houses was at Sharpham House near Totnes, planned as the show home of Captain Philemon Pownoll, and financed with Spanish gold captured in the Seven Years' War. The most prestigious architects, artists and furniture makers were employed to create an outstanding estate. Paintings of the site from 1769 seem to suggest alternative layouts from which Pownoll could choose his preferred layout of the landscape when work began in 1770. A carriage route circled the estate, leading through woodland along the river bank to an artificially dammed lake. Here an octagonal tower, known as the Pleasure House, could be found with two small adjacent buildings – the boathouse and the bathing house. An open-air plunge pool lay in front of the bathing house on a rocky promontory, fed with salt water from the river. The bathing house served as a changing room and refreshment would have been taken in the Pleasure House behind – an elegant Georgian room, finely plastered, with a fireplace and Italianate windows offering panoramic views of the winding river below. The artificial lake offered the possibility of fishing or sailing a small boat. A day could be passed here with *al fresco* meals and entertainment for a small group of family or friends, away from the constraints of life in the mansion on the hill above. The surprise of arriving at the riverside setting to find the Pleasure House, concealed in the trees, revealing nothing of the delights within, must have transformed this location into a place of fantasy and secret delights. The experience of driving away at the end of the day in a carriage across the causeway between

William Payne's 'sublime' representation of Sharpham soon after the completion of the estate. (Westcountry Studies Library)

the lake and the river would have been memorable.

By the nineteenth century bathing houses had ceased to be the preserve of the aristocracy, as is shown by a small Regency marine villa near the mouth of the River Dart known as 'The Wilderness'. Possibly by this date, salt water bathing was no longer a novelty, since The Wilderness ignores the plentiful supply of salt water available locally and utilises fresh spring water instead. Built around 1820 for a Dr William Cholwich Hunt, the

Sharpham House, on the Dart, Devonshire.

An 1834 etching after the bathing house was demolished and the pool built over. By 1842 it provided accommodation for a gamekeeper and his family. (Westcountry Studies Library)

villa was designed for a well-to-do professional gentleman, with seven bedrooms, plus one for a manservant. A precipitous slope rises straight out of the Dart, with remarkable views, and at the bottom of a steeply sloping terraced garden are a bathing house and a boathouse. The small stone two-storey building is in the Gothick style with a room on each floor. The upper room contains a fireplace and a window in the north-east wall taking full advantage of the river views. A glazed arched door in the south-east wall leads onto a small stone balcony with a very fine cast-iron balustrade. Downstairs the walls are cut into the stone cliff, and spring water issues from an alcove in the rockwork in a continuous small stream into the room itself; possibly a stone trough or a cast-iron bath caught the water for bathing.

Situated just above high water level, the spring water running through the bathing house seeps out onto the rock face into the river below.

The Wilderness. Advertised for sale in 1867, the bathing house was still sufficiently noteworthy to be mentioned in the sale notice in an area prized for its bathing provisions. (B. Rolf)

PUBLIC SEAWATER
BATHING HOUSES

O WNERS OF PRIVATE ESTATES on coasts and estuaries were not the only
people to see the possibilities for health and enjoyment in the new
seawater bathing fashion, and public facilities began to appear in the second
half of the eighteenth century, although they were not common until the
nineteenth century. The Portsmouth baths, situated in Bath Square, must have
been a successful facility, since a hotel was later built next door for the bath
house patrons, and the name Quebec House adopted to commemorate the
battle fought in 1759. Lake Taswell's *The Portsmouth Guide*, published in 1775,
describes the provisions of Quebec House:

> In 1754, was built by subscription of the inhabitants, a large and commodious
> bathing-house, containing four fine baths of different depths of water, two
> of them large enough to swim in. It is situated near the mouth of the harbour,
> close to the run of the tide, and every flood is plentifully supplied with water.
> In it are two good dressing-rooms, one for the gentlemen, one for the ladies,
> with every other necessary accommodation.

It seems likely that this sophisticated operation evolved from a simpler
provision dating from 1735, when Joseph Bucknall leased the beach on the
site of Quebec House, with bathing rights and the right to build bathing huts
for 1,000 years. It is not possible to establish what class of patrons used
Quebec House, for Bath Square and this area of Portsmouth Point generally
had a highly coloured reputation: Thomas Rowlandson's contemporary
paintings depict the Navy drinking and carousing whilst ashore there.

Daniel Defoe visited nearby Lymington in 1727, recording that 'rogueing
and smuggling' were the major industries. By the mid-1750s, the town
became a little more genteel and boasted two salt water bathing
establishments, with the proprietor of one being fined 4d for failing to pay
rates on his business. Thomas Rowlandson visited the town in 1784 and
painted a view entitled *Mrs Beeston's Baths*, showing a random collection of
buildings on the edge of the sea marsh, probably around 1780, where

Opposite:
A watercolour
view showing the
new Lymington
bath house
in 1833.

45

Quebec House: a rare early example of the new breed of bath houses was built at Portsmouth Point in Hampshire, funded by public subscription.

Plans by Lymington Council to demolish the baths in 1946 were luckily shelved and the building survives today as Lymington Town Sailing Club.

'strengthening sea baths' were available. Possibly the baths were taken in the river itself, since in 1825 the cost of a cold water bath was 6d, while the same facility with 'a guide' cost 1s; the purpose of the guide was to stop the client sinking by means of a rope tied under the armpits. Mrs Beeston's Baths were replaced when, in an attempt to:

…maintain and raise [Lymington's] character as a watering-place, a public company was formed on the 10th March, 1833, under the name of the 'Lymington Bath and Improvement Company', having for its objects the erection of more commodious baths, the enclosure of a considerable tract of mudland, and the improving of the approaches to the bathing establishments.

Built in a neo-classical style, the central building was hexagonal, with an upper floor for social gatherings, and a ground floor vaulted entrance hall which echoed the design of the subterranean baths below, where salt water flowed in at every high tide and was heated in the boilers. Hot, cold and 'vapour' bathing was available, with separate wings of the building catering for 'ladies and gentlemen.' Outside was an extensive open-air salt swimming

Bathing machines and indoor salt water baths co-existed happily at Budleigh Salterton (left), with more grandiose arrangements at Torquay (below) providing a swimming pool approximately 15 metres square, filling through arched colonnades from the sea. (Westcountry Studies Library)

The Pump House. Supposedly health-giving water was pumped from Haslar Creek via this building up to Anglesey Gardens.

pool. Unfortunately, this optimistic scheme failed to halt Lymington's decline as a resort and money problems set in from 1855. By the 1940s the bath house was in a state of dilapidation following a period as a coastguard lookout and as a telegraph office.

Part of Lymington's decline as a fashionable resort was echoed at Alverstoke, also in Hampshire, on the west side of Portsmouth Harbour. An ambitious scheme was launched in 1826 to develop a select seaside resort, named Angleseyville, rivalling Brighton. An imposing double crescent of houses in the neo-classical style, together with a handful of marine villas,

Angleseyville was named after its dashing patron the Marquis of Anglesey, previously involved in a speculative development at Caernarvon Castle in Wales where the central tower in this picture was converted into public seawater baths. (Landmark Trust)

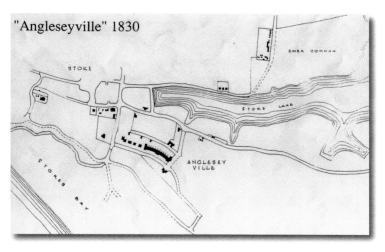

"Angleseyville" 1830

Plans from 1830 show the proposed development with the Reading Room/Bath Houses in the gardens opposite The Crescent. (Wendy Osborne and the Friends of Anglesey Gardens)

a hotel, race course and private gardens housing a reading room and bath houses were planned as a speculative development. Only half of the crescent was actually built, but the attendant attractions were provided for people wishing to restore their health and enjoy themselves in a refined setting. The private gardens allowed holidaymakers who were able to pay the subscription to enjoy their surroundings, strolling along the raised terrace walkway on the seaward side with extensive views across to the Isle of Wight and out to the Navy anchorage at Spithead. The whole concept might have been based

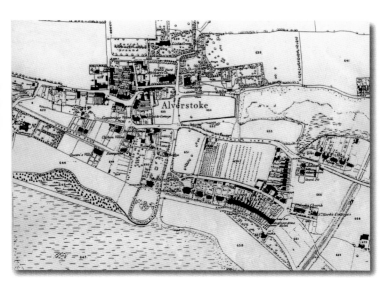

While only a limited commercial success because it did not capitalise early enough on the salt water bathing fashion, this 1870 plan shows how attractive Angleseyville proved. (Wendy Osborne and the Friends of Anglesey Gardens)

Demolished in 1950, this 1920s photograph shows the Reading Room entrance and flanking Bath Houses at Angleseyville. (Lesley Burton and the Gosport Society)

Opposite top: New Baths, Plymouth. In 1766 the baths, assembly room, bowling green and promenade with gardens and seats provided the nucleus of the seaside attractions in Plymouth.

Opposite middle: By 1825 the Royal Clarence Baths provided hot and cold baths, showers, vapour baths and swimming pools, with sea bathing also available from the beach.

on Jane Austen's unfinished novel *Sanditon*, and, indeed, her brother Admiral Sir Charles Austen lived here in one of the marine villas and worked actively to support the developer's plans to raise more capital to complete the project.

Entering the Bath House complex through a pillared portico, patrons climbed stairs to the elevated Reading Room at the rear, overlooking the Solent, or used the baths in the adjoining wings. The 1841 Census recorded a gardener, Henry Cooper, and his wife, 'a labourer', who lived in the basement beneath the reading room, keeping the gardens tidy and presumably stoking the boilers to provide warm salt water as required. Also housed in the basement was a large water reservoir for the baths and, in the adjacent gardens, several subterranean, brick soakaways, which allowed the salt water to run away from the baths through ceramic pipes into the nearby ha-ha; this prevented grazing animals from invading the well-kept gardens. Although the Bath House was demolished in 1950, the Pump House, which supplied sufficient head of pressure to lift the water from Haslar Creek, still remains, providing reliable evidence for the architectural appearance of the bath house itself. An advertisement in the *Hampshire Telegraph* for 27 June 1831 mentions:

> Warm and Cold Baths, with an elegant Reading Room, situate in a beautiful Promenade; also Machine Baths, on the clear and delightful beach of Stokes Bay.

Angleseyville's big selling point was that invalids and delicate children could enjoy all the benefits of sea air and salt water while staying a safe distance from the overly bracing breezes of the actual beach.

A View of the New Baths and Long Room near Plymouth 1766.

A. Long Room.   D. Seats for Pleasure   G. Coach Road through Stonehouse. K. Plymouth Sound.
B. Baths.   E. Entrance to the Bowling Green. H. Fine Lawn.   L. Mount Edgcomb.
C. Convenient Houses.   F. Mount Stone.   I. Mill Bay.   M. Fields et cetera, &c.

Drawn from Nature & on Stone by H. Worsley.   Printed by C. Hullmandel.

ROYAL UNION BATHS, PLYMOUTH.

Left: £10,000 was raised from shares to finance the Royal Union Baths in 1828. Hot fresh- and salt-water baths were provided, and two swimming pools (one for ladies) in addition to sulpherous fumigating and hot air baths. (All three images on this page are courtesy of Westcountry Studies Library)

51

RETRIEVING THE INVISIBLE

Following a typical
eighteenth-century
pattern, in 1767
Cams estate
passed to Sir Jacob
Wolff. Newly
married and
created a baronet,
he commissioned
the building of a
fine Palladian
mansion, with
extensive views of
Portsmouth
Harbour.

WHILE MANY bathing houses and plunge pools have simply disappeared from view as they fell into disuse, some can be retrieved from obscurity because they were recorded in documents or paintings.

There has been a manor house at the Cams estate on Fareham Creek in Hampshire since the thirteenth century. By 1770 the estate was sold to Brigadier General John Carnac, late of the East India Company. On his remarriage, Carnac followed the previous owner's plans for 'improving' the estate and Cams became one of many grand 'Nabob' houses. Money problems forced his return to India in 1774 and the estate passed to the local Delme family in 1783. An ex-Lord Mayor of London and Director of the Bank of England, Peter Delme owned three country houses together with a house in Grosvenor Square. With a retinue of a hundred servants, numerous mistresses, horses and his own pack of hounds, money problems had become pressing at the time of his death in 1789. His wife, Lady Betty, set about restoring the family fortunes, marrying her son, John, into a local family in 1791, and consolidating this success with her own

marriage into the same family in 1794. John wrought further improvements to the estate on his marriage, creating an impressively long drive to the Palladian mansion through immaculate gardens, and, probably at this time, building the bathing house with a walled, outdoor plunge pool, set amongst woodland on the banks of Fareham Creek. Only the footings of the bathing house and plunge pool survive today, but the woodland is now in a conservation area known as Bathing House Coppice. The estate suffered a decline common to many grand mansions in the twentieth century, with the house requisitioned by the Ministry of Defence during the Second World War and the stables, orangery, walled gardens, hot houses and bathing house all falling into decay. A disastrous explosion at a nearby armaments depot in 1950 hastened the decline of the mansion until it was restored by a development company in the 1990s. Their

The Orangery: even the domestic buildings on the estate displayed the status of the owner.

Wooden stakes outline parallel breakwaters, probably filled with large chunks of stone and turfed on top to provide a landing stage on three sides of the plunge pool, providing moorings for boats bringing supplies to Cams Hall at

historical report on the estate noted 'an angular causeway of stone built into the creek. Bath house at inland end, probably to house a bathing machine.' This was the commonly held view, although evidence on the ground pointed to a bathing house giving access to a sloping brick causeway running down to a large plunge pool in the creek itself, filling with salt water at high tide. The re-emergence in 2005 of a fine oil painting by local artist, Hayter Kinch, dating from 1830, proved conclusively that this was, in fact, the case. One of a pair of landscapes of Fareham Creek, both paintings show not only the private bath house of the Delme family, but also the little public bath house on the opposite bank sited at the end of Bathing House Lane (now Bath Lane).

In terms of actual remains, even less survives of the bathing house at Abbotsbury Castle, on Chesil Beach, Dorset, but letters, maps and postcards allow the reconstruction of a building belonging to another family whose estates reflected their prestige and social status. Known also as Strangways Castle, after the family who built it, Abbotsbury was a style statement from its inception. The Strangways owned a hunting lodge in the village of Abbotsbury, but by the 1760s the enthusiasm for sea bathing influenced their decision to build a 'sham' castle directly above Chesil Beach, overlooking the sea. Charles Hamilton, whose extensive pleasure grounds at Painshill in Surrey created a reputation for their owner before eventually bankrupting him, advised the Strangways on their seaside residence, but the project seems to have been undertaken mostly to satisfy Elizabeth Strangways Horner, the first Countess of Ilchester. Lord Ilchester wrote to Henry Fox in 1748 that his wife had taken their children to Abbotsbury 'upon a supposition that the sea air is good, which to be sure is nonsense.'

Lady Ilchester's letter to a friend in 1766 suggests that she financed the building from her own considerable wealth:

Hayter Kinch's 1830 painting showing the Cams Hall bathing house and jetty on the left bank of Fareham Creek and the public baths at the end of Bathing House Lane on the right-hand bank. (Hampshire County Council Museums and Archives Service)

I have been a jaunt to my new house, Pin Money Castle. It is close to the sea, which is a most noble and awfull sight as there was a most remarkable high south wind.

The bathing house at Abbotsbury (plus awning in front). Until the mid-eighteenth century most buildings would have occupied a sheltered position, unlike Abbotsbury where 'the sea prospect [was] very grand and seen from the drawing room window as though we had been on board a ship.' (D. Stevens)

The Earl and Countess of Ilchester seem to have been plunge pool enthusiasts: both had travelled extensively in Europe before their marriage, and cold baths existed at two of their country estates in Somerset before 1750. Their enthusiasm transmitted itself to the next generation who, having been used to cold plunge baths at home and salt water baths on holidays in Wales, built bathing houses for themselves at Penrice, on the Gower, and at Abbotsbury Castle. Just as unusual as the position of Abbotsbury Castle was the position of the 'neat bathing house' built right on Chesil Beach itself in 1791 by the second Earl. Matching the castle in style, with Gothick doors and long windows, the building comprised hot and cold baths and a dressing room.

Commanding breathtaking views across Lyme Bay to the west, and along Chesil Beach and the Fleet salt lagoon to Portland in the east, Abbotsbury Castle was in the forefront of the fashion for marine residences.

Ascot (above) and Painshill (below) are both currently undergoing restoration. (Ascot by permission of the owners of Ascot Place; Painshill by permission of Painshill Park Trust)

Providing a hot bath is a more complex operation than directing a cold natural spring into a plunge pool, requiring fuel for the boiler and servants to supervise the heating process. Abbotsbury bathing house sits on the beach below and slightly to the west of the Castle, adjacent to several farm buildings and cottages attached to the estate. A spring rises in the cliff there, presumably the reason for siting 'Laundry Cottage' at that point (at one time it probably handled the laundry from the Castle). A boiler on site would have provided the laundry with the necessary hot water, and probably fed the bath house just across the lane. Salt water, if required, would have been brought up in buckets from the sea. The position of the bathing house, now little more than a bush-covered depression in the shingle, can be established by maps from the early nineteenth century. Destroyed by fire in 1913, the Castle was rebuilt but subsequently demolished when subsidence caused the building to shift down the hillside.

The grotto and bath at Oatlands Park, Surrey has also gone, but its beauty can be retrieved through written accounts and from remaining grottoes built

by the Lane family. Started in 1747 and costing around £40,000, this sophisticated enterprise was designed for the 9th Earl of Lincoln. Its complex design made it seem even larger than its 18-metre length. It comprised three rooms on the ground floor: the First Chamber decorated with clam shells and glittering artificial stalactites, a Gaming Room in the Chinese style, encrusted also with shell and stalactites; and with a fireplace and chandelier; and finally the Bath Chamber where a statue of Venus de Medici presided over a deep, spring-fed bath amid a riot of shell decoration. Upper rooms, full of sunshine and quite different to the cool gloom of the ground floor, were used for meals. Oatlands passed later to the Duke and Duchess of York, and over a century of use by several owners the grotto changed in style and use, but always contained a fantastic riot of decoration. It must have produced a magical atmosphere when decorated by candlelight, with the sound of water running over the cascade and into the plunge pool.

The grotto and bath at Oatlands is thought to have been the work of the Lane family from Wiltshire, who seem to have been grotto builders for half a century, reputedly involved at Stourhead, Old Wardour Castle, Painshill and Ascot Place. Destroyed in 1948 by the local council together with the Ministry of Works and claimed to be a dangerous structure, the building still took four days to be demolished with pneumatic drills.

Painshill today suggests the delights of Oatlands, where Charles Greville recorded 'I bathed in the cold bath in the grotto, which is as clear as crystal and as cold as ice.' (By permission of Painshill Park Trust)

THE SEAMY SIDE

THE APPEARANCE and size of many bath houses and plunge pools suggest that they were used just as an aid to health by their owners. The plunge pools at Corsham and at Elbury Cove are small and shallow, allowing their owners, at best, the opportunity to squat down and immerse the body briefly in cold water. Others appear as mini swimming pools – Greenway, Cams Hall, Erddig in Wales – where a longer immersion and some physical activity could have been undertaken in rather bracing surroundings. A third category hints at bathing as a sociable activity in luxurious surroundings. Wynnstay in Denbighshire had an outdoor pool the size of a large swimming bath with a substantial Roman-style changing room alongside. This suggests that the owner's chums from his Grand Tour days may have joined him there and reminisced in suitably civilised surroundings.

These differing styles suggest that modes of use were as varied, and sometimes as eccentric, as their owners, and that the bath was not always the venue where health might be improved, or for an uplifting encounter with nature in a sublime setting, but hint more at an attitude to bathing which was apparent in Ancient Rome. Once the fear of plague, which decimated fourteenth-century Europe and was spread partly by communal bathing, was finally laid to rest in the more relaxed attitudes of the eighteenth century, bathing re-appeared. The aristocracy, with their passionate interest in classical ideals, would have been well aware of the central importance of both private and public baths in Ancient Greece and Rome, prized as much for their social importance as for cleanliness, and elements of this appear in the recreational aspects of many eighteenth-century British bathing houses. Kedleston, Greenway, Sharpham, Walton, Elbury Cove and Carshalton are amongst many boasting elegant drawing rooms with beautiful views, where refreshments were taken in convivial surroundings. If the bath itself provided a short, sharp shock, it was not the entire experience.

The public baths of Ancient Rome also served a less salubrious purpose. Graffiti and wall paintings at Pompeii and Herculaneum still display evidence that the sex trade often flourished at these locations. And so it proved in

Opposite:
One of the less salacious of the satirical cartoons circulating amongst high society, by James Gillray (1776–1815), depicts events at the Maidstone bath house. (British Museum)

59

Remains of the
Painshill plunge
pool, once a
circular Roman-
style thatched
building, awaiting
restoration.
(By permission
of Painshill Park
Trust)

Georgian London, particularly in the area around the Piazza of Covent Garden, also known as the Great Square of Venus. Here actresses and courtesans frequented the taverns, coffee houses and *bagnios* where every form of human frailty was catered for. William Hogarth depicted this life vividly in his paintings, with scene five of *Marriage a la Mode* showing the Earl dying after a duel with his wife's lover in an upstairs room of the Turk's Head *bagnio*. Many of the Covent Garden *bagnios* offered no bathing facilities; the name was just a useful cover. Others were luxuriously appointed and offered bathing facilities amongst a multitude of other services, like that frequented by the Italian adventurer Casanova:

> In the evening I frequented the most select bagnios where a man of quality can sup, bathe, and meet well-bred women of easy virtue. There are plenty of this sort in London. The entertainment only costs about six guineas, and with economy one can do it for four; but economy was never one of my failings.

This ambivalence towards certain types of baths was obviously well established in the eighteenth-century mind, as revealed by a high-profile court case centred on the cold baths at Maidstone. These were visited in the summer of 1778 by Sir Richard and Lady Seymour Worsley, in company with their friend George Bisset, who was also Seymour's lover. Seymour was a regular visitor to the baths and the party used the separate pools provided for men and women. Seymour took longer to get dressed after her bath, and the men waiting outside decided that Sir Richard should hoist Bisset onto his shoulders to enable him to spy through a high window on Lady Worsley as she emerged from the bath. The accommodating Sir Richard supported Bisset for five minutes while Seymour Worsley displayed herself to her lover. This high-spirited frolic later became the basis of evidence for a divorce when Seymour absconded with Bisset in 1781. Taking the unusual step of divorce proceedings against his wife, Worsley demanded the huge sum of £20,000 in damages from the lovers. Evidence from the bath attendant proved the complicity of all three involved in the case, and their fall from society was complete. With Queen Victoria's accession in 1837, a more modest and decorous age dawned, shunning the robust fashions of Georgian society, and bathing houses and plunge pools began to slip slowly into obscurity.

FURTHER READING

Ashenburg, Katherine. *Clean: An Unsanitised History of Washing*. Profile Books, 2008.

Batey, Mavis. *Alexander Pope: the Poet and the Landscape*. Barn Elms, 1999.

Cruickshank, Dan. *The Secret History of Georgian London*. RH Books, 2009.

Day, Angélique (ed.). *Letters from Georgian Ireland: The Correspondence of Mary Delaney, 1713–68*. Friar's Bush Press, 1991.

Girouard, Mark. *Life in the English Country House*. Penguin Books, 1980.

Harris, John. *The Palladian Revival: Lord Burlington, His Villa and Garden at Chiswick*. Yale University Press, 1995.

Hunt, John Dixon and Willis, Peter (eds.). *The Genius of the Place: The English Landscape Garden 1620–1820*. Paul Elek, 1975.

Jones, Barbara. *Follies and Grottoes*. Constable, 2nd edition, 1974.

Martin, Joanna. *Wives and Daughters: Women and Children in the Georgian Country House*. Hambledon and London, 2004.

Miller, Naomi. *Heavenly Caves: Reflections on the Garden Grotto*. George Braziller, 1982.

Mowl, Timothy. *William Kent: Architect, Designer, Opportunist*. Jonathan Cape, 2006.

Rubenhold, Hallie. *Lady Worsley's Whim*. Chatto & Windus, 2008.

Strong, Roy. *The Artist and the Garden*. Yale University Press, 2000.

Turner, Roger. *Capability Brown and the Eighteenth-Century English Landscape*. Phillimore, 2nd edition, 1999.

Woodbridge, Kenneth. *The Stourhead Landscape*. National Trust, 2002.

GAZETTEER

Although many bathing houses and plunge pools still exist, some are on private estates inaccessible to the public, and others are in a ruinous condition. All the bathing houses and plunge pools listed here can be viewed by the public, although access in some cases is strictly limited and needs to be arranged in advance with the owner or custodian. In some cases only the exteriors may be viewed since the buildings have been converted for other purposes. The Folly Fellowship has compiled and published an exhaustive and authoritative gazetteer of all bathing houses, both private and public, traced to date (www.follies.org.uk). Three of the bath houses mentioned in the book are administered by the Landmark Trust (www.landmarktrust.co.uk) as holiday homes.

Albury Park, Albury, Guildford, Surrey GU5 9BB.
Telephone: 01483 202323
(only open two weekends a year under the National Gardens Scheme)
Antony House, Torpoint, Cornwall PL11 2QA.
Telephone: 01752 812191 (National Trust)
Arno's Court Bath House, Portmeirion, Gwynned, N. Wales LL48 6ET.
Telephone: 01766 770000.
Website: www.portmeirion-village.com (privately owned)
Bateman's Tower, Waterside, Brightlingsea, Essex.
Bath Tower, Caernarvon, Wales. Landmark Trust, Shottesbrooke,
Maidenhead, Berkshire, SL6 3SW.
Telephone: 01628 825925. Website: www.landmarktrust.org.uk
Boconnoc House, Lostwithiel, Cornwall PL22 ORG.
Telephone: 01208 872507. Website: www.boconnocenterprises.co.uk
Carshalton Water Tower, Pound Street, Carshalton, Surrey SM5 3PN.
Telephone: 020 8643 3377. Website: www.carshaltonwatertower.co.uk
Chatsworth, Bakewell, Derbyshire DE45 1PE.
Telephone: 01246 582204. Website: www.chatsworth.org
Cleveland Pools, Hampton Row, Bath, Somerset.
Corsham Court, Corsham, Wiltshire SN13 OBZ.
Telephone: 01249 701610. Website: www.corsham-court.co.uk
(privately owned)
Duke's Bath House, Beaulieu, Brockenhurst, Hampshire SO42 7ZN.
Telephone: 01590 614605. Website: wwwbeaulieu.co.uk (privately
owned)
Greenway, Greenway Rd, Galmpton, Devon TQ5 0ES.
Telephone: 01803 842382 (National Trust)
Holyrood House, Abbeyhill, Edinburgh, Scotland EH8 8DX.
Telephone: 0131 556 5100. Website: www.royalcollection.org.uk
Kedleston Hall, Nr. Quarndon, Derby, Derbyshire DE22 5JH.
Telephone: 01332 842191 (National Trust)
Kenwood House, Hampstead Lane, London NW3 7JR.
Telephone: 020 7973 3507. Website: www.english-heritage.org.uk
Lymington Town Sailing Club, Bath Rd, Lymington, Hampshire SO4 13SE.
Telephone: 01590 674 514. Website: www.ltsc.co.uk
Mount Edgcumbe, Cremyll, Torpoint, Cornwall PL10 1HZ.
Telephone: 01752 822236.
Website: www.cornwalltouristboard.co.uk/mountedgcumbe
Packwood House, Packwood Lane, Lapworth, Warwickshire B94 6AT.
Telephone: 01564 783294 (National Trust)
Painshill Park, Portsmouth Rd, Cobham, Surrey KT11 1JE.
Telephone: 01932 868113. Website: www.painshill.co.uk

Painswick Rococo Gardens, Painswick, Gloucestershire GL6 6TH.
    Telephone: 01452 813204. Website: www.rococogarden.co.uk
Pentillie Castle, St Mellion, Saltash, Cornwall PL12 6QD.
    Telephone: 01579 350044. Website: www.pentillie.co.uk
    (privately owned)
Princess Amelia's Bath House, Gunnersbury Park, Pope's Lane, London
    W3 8LQ. Telephone: 020 8992 1612.
    Website: www.gunnersburyparkcovenant.co.uk
Quebec House, Bath Square, Old Portsmouth, Hampshire PO1 2JL
    (privately owned)
Raby Castle, Nr. Barnard Castle, Darlington, Co. Durham DL2 3AH.
    Telephone: 01833 660202. Website: www.rabycastle.com
Ranger's House, Chesterfield Walk, Greenwich, London SE10 8QX.
    Telephone: 020 8853 0035.
'Roman' Bath, 5 Strand Lane, London WC2. Telephone: 020 7641 5264.
'Roman' Baths, The Nook, Stoney Middleton, Derbyshire.
Rousham, Nr. Steeple Aston, Bicester, Oxfordshire OX25 4QX.
    Telephone: 01869 347110.
    Website: www.rousham.org (privately owned)
St Winifred's Well, Flint, Wales. Landmark Trust, Shottesbrooke,
    Maidenhead, Berkshire, SL6 3SW.
    Telephone: 01628 825920. Website: www.landmarktrust.org.uk
Stourhead, Stourton, Warminster, Wiltshire BA12 6QD.
    Telephone: 01747 841152 (National Trust)
Walton, Nr. Stratford-upon-Avon, Warwickshire. Landmark Trust,
    Shottesbrooke, Maidenhead, Berkshire, SL6 3SW.
    Telephone: 01628 825920. Website: www.landmarktrust.org.uk
Warnford Park, Warnford, Hampshire SO32 3LF. (The park is only open
    to the public on Sunday afternoons in February.)
Wimpole Hall, Arrington, Royston, Cambridgeshire SG8 0BW.
    Telephone: 01223 206000 (National Trust)
Wrest Park, Silsoe, Bedfordshire MK45 4HS. Telephone: 01525 860152.
    Website: www.english-heritage.org.uk (English Heritage)

INDEX